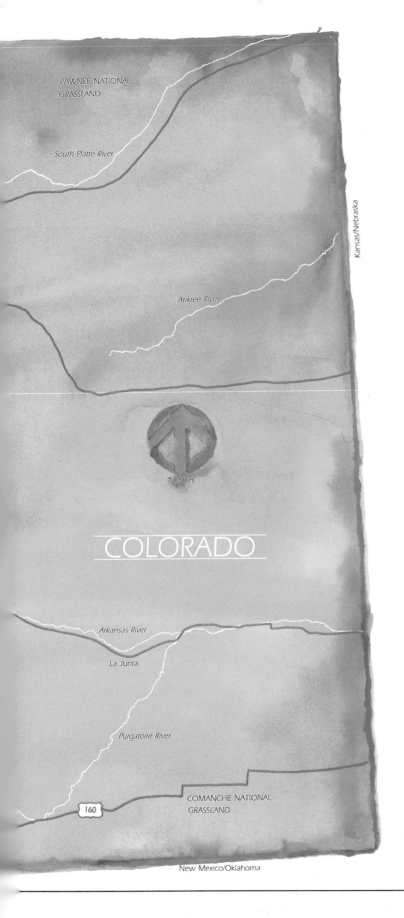

PAWNEE NATIONAL
GRASSLAND

South Platte River

Arikree River

Kansas/Nebraska

NORTH

COLORADO

Arkansas River

La Junta

Purgatoire River

160

COMANCHE NATIONAL
GRASSLAND

New Mexico/Oklahoma

EXISTING WILDERNESS AREAS IN COLORADO

PR :	PLATTE RIVER
MZ :	MOUNT ZIRKEL
R :	RAWAH
CLP :	CACHE LA POUDRE
CP :	COMANCHE PEAK
N :	NEOTA
NS :	NEVER SUMMER
IP :	INDIAN PEAKS
FT :	FLAT TOPS
EN :	EAGLES NEST
ME :	MOUNT EVANS
HC :	HOLY CROSS
LC :	LOST CREEK
HF :	HUNTER - FRYING PAN
MM :	MOUNT MASSIVE
MS :	MAROON BELLS - SNOWMASS
COP :	COLLEGIATE PEAKS
RA :	RAGGEDS
WE :	WEST ELK
*BC :	BLACK CANYON OF THE GUNNISON
MTS :	MOUNT SNEFFELS
LH :	LIZARD HEAD
W :	WEMINUCHE
BB :	BIG BLUE
LG :	LA GARITA
*MV :	MESA VERDE
SS :	SOUTH SAN JUAN
*GS :	GREAT SAND DUNES

* NATIONAL PARK SERVICE LAND

S0-AJV-239

FOSSIL RIDGE	13. BIG BLUE ADDITIONS	17. WEST NEEDLES
ROUBIDEAU	14. WHEELER GEOLOGIC	18. PIEDRA
TABEGUACHE	15. SANGRE DE CRISTO	19. SPANISH PEAKS
CANNIBAL PLATEAU–POWDERHORN	16. GREENHORN MOUNTAIN	20. SOUTH SAN JUAN

COLORADO
OUR WILDERNESS FUTURE

PROPOSED ADDITIONS
TO THE WILDERNESS SYSTEM

PHOTOGRAPHY BY JOHN FIELDER

WESTCLIFFE PUBLISHERS, INC.   ENGLEWOOD, COLORADO

CONTENTS

International Standard Book Number: ISBN 0-929969-38-3

Library of Congress Catalogue Card Number: 90-083683

Copyright, Photographs and Text: Westcliffe Publishers, Inc.

Editor: John Fielder   *333.782*

Assistant Editor: Margaret Terrell Morse   *FIE*

Production Manager: Mary Jo Lawrence   *3.9f*

Typographer: Ruth Koning

Map: Ann W. Douden

Color Separations by: Greg Walz, Spectrum, Inc., Golden, Colorado

Printed in Colorado by Mountain West Printing Co., Inc., Denver

Printed on recycled paper

Published by Westcliffe Publishers, Inc.

    2650 South Zuni Street, Englewood, Colorado 80110

First frontispiece: Lupine and Indian paintbrush wildflowers, Oh! Be Joyful proposed addition to the Raggeds Wilderness

Title page: Patterns in rock below Pettingell Peak, Williams Fork proposed wilderness

Right: Early winter storm coats all in its way, on the flanks of Mount Blaine, proposed addition to the Lost Creek Wilderness

TIM WIRTH

FOREWORD

For hundreds of years the Rocky Mountains have provided the image that defines life in this part of the West. The mountains have inspired awe from visitor and settler alike.

Although the Rockies were a formidable obstacle to westward expansion, even many of the early pioneers were astounded by their beauty. "This veuw is wurth all my pane and trubble and sufring," a man from Indiana wrote in his journal while crossing the Rocky Mountains about 140 years ago.

Today a view of the Rocky Mountains is as good as it was then, and it's available without the pain and trouble and suffering. The view has changed in places as we have built roads, towns, ranches and reservoirs, but the mountains are still here and the view is still spectacular.

An appreciation of the landscape has been part of the western experience since the first pioneers reached Colorado. Americans have never sat around waiting for John Muir and the Sierra Club to come along and teach them how to enjoy nature. Such appreciation has been shared by all who live here or have ever been here.

The story of America's westward expansion as told by those who made the journey is full of references to the beauty and grandeur of the Rocky Mountains. These were people who were pressed to the limits of their resources, uncertain of their future and even their survival, yet they found the energy to sit and write in their journals. They wrote about their hardships, they wrote about their dreams for the future and they wrote about the beauty of nature which they witnessed every day. "Oh, beautiful is the hand of nature," wrote Lucena Parsons in 1850. "I hate to leave these beauties, but must on."

Over and over in the journals of the people who settled the West, we find the desire to spend more time right here, walking in the mountains, absorbing these scenes. Most of them, though, kept moving, heading for a friendlier climate and for settlements where life would be easier.

Elizabeth Dixon Smith, traveling to Oregon with her husband and eight children, passed over the Rockies in 1847 and took the time to describe the scene in her journal. "It is all rocks on top and they are split in to pieces and turned edgeways. Oh, that I had time and talent to describe this curious country."

Most of the people who passed through Colorado in the last century did not have the time to explore the landscape. They did not have the luxuries of cities, highways, cars, Coleman stoves and goose down sleeping bags. Still, they took the time to record their thoughts, and they left us a record of appreciation for the mountain landscape.

Today we do have the time to explore the wilderness, and we have the means to do so comfortably and with little risk. We can drive to campgrounds and trailheads. We can put on Gore-Tex hiking boots and head into the wilderness on well-constructed and well-maintained trails. At the end of the day, we have the option of retreating to a luxury resort hotel or a quaint bed and breakfast. We can have our cake and eat it too.

What would we say to Elizabeth Smith and Lucena Parsons if we were to meet them today? Would we tell them we didn't allow ourselves time to enjoy nature? Would we tell them instead that we spent our time utterly transforming — sometimes even erasing — the landscape that had moved them so?

When we look back at the generations that settled Colorado, we find a legacy of love and stewardship for the land. There is a well-established American tradition — a tradition easy to forget — of regular people who took nature seriously, who yearned to know more about the natural settings they could only catch glimpses of.

The people of Colorado's past were not a social monolith devoted solely to economic development. They were not a wave of humanity single-mindedly pursuing profit at the expense of other human values. Our ancestors in Colorado bequeathed us a strong and deep-rooted tradition of loving nature. We owe them the justice of recognizing this.

We owe these people nothing less than to treat the land they left us with respect. This land is our heritage. It is where we came from, and it is where our children and their children will live long after we are gone.

Imagine a people that has destroyed its past and you see a people without a future. Just as it has been necessary to use and develop much of the planet, it is also necessary to save some of it in a natural state.

The preservation of wilderness is not a rejection of human existence. Rather, it is a distinctly human thing to do. In the interest of society's common good, we need highways, farms, cities and developed campgrounds. We also need to designate some lands to be left alone so that we might always have the same pleasure of observing natural beauty that our ancestors had.

Wilderness in Colorado is more than just a good idea, more than just a noble attempt to preserve something of our past. It is a resource that can be used for the benefit of Coloradans. Some of us find deep pleasure in being able to hike into the wilderness; for others, it is enough to see these areas from the comfort of an automobile.

For all of us, wilderness means jobs. Tourism is one of the most important industries in the state, and tourists want to see wilderness. When people around the country think about Colorado, they think about mountains and rivers. It is because of our natural splendor that people come to Colorado.

It is good to build highways, airports, convention centers and resorts. We need these things. Without them, we would have a difficult time attracting visitors and new businesses. But we have to remember that it is our wilderness that people come for.

When we go into the wilderness we are faced with something larger than ourselves, something that will last longer than we will last. To lose that is to lose perspective.

This generation of Coloradans will be remembered for how it deals with the wilderness questions. Future generations will look back and know that we either preserved their heritage or squandered it.

— TIM WIRTH
U.S. Senator, Colorado

THOMAS A. BARRON

INTRODUCTION

Mountain water whispers, splashing over shining stones, gurgling and bubbling through this alpine meadow like a trail of liquid sky. Wind rises at my back, bearing the fragrance of eagle's nest and ragged canyon, sweet sage and snowy peak. Colorado wilderness surrounds me, and I take a deep breath of cold, crystalline air.

I sit upon an ancient slab of rock, wet from the misty spray of the stream, and study the endlessly interwoven patterns of lichen on its face. I wonder what this rock has witnessed over the stretch of geologic time: ages when the earth, still young and savage, surged skyward and split apart, collapsed, cooled, sagged to support an inland ocean, rose again as the waters receded, flamed and froze, buckled and folded, cracked and compressed, trembled with the footsteps of dinosaurs, received the dying dinosaurs' bones, fought against advancing glaciers, saw them melt into turquoise lakes, hardened into a ridge whose melting snows spawned this coursing stream that has quenched the Ute huntsman's thirst and fed the flowers of 10,000 Julys.

Then, in the wet soil by the stream, I spot a single paw print. Might it be a mountain lion?

Along with many other Coloradans, I feel lucky to have experienced a few moments like this in the still-wild places portrayed in this magnificent book by John Fielder. I hope that many more people will also have the opportunity to experience these places — but that is by no means a certainty. A fierce battle is being fought over some of Colorado's most important wild areas, a battle that will decide whether they are to be ultimately opened for development or protected, intact, for all time.

The battle is over whether these lands, the 20 remarkable places depicted in John Fielder's unforgettable photographs,

will be designated as wilderness areas under the National Wilderness Preservation System. Together they comprise 841,280 acres, little more than *1 percent* of Colorado's total land area. But their relatively small size does not mean that the controversy surrounding them is also small. It is large, it is heated and it is likely to be resolved one way or another in the near future.

To understand the Colorado wilderness battle, we must know something about the lands that are at stake — and at risk. We must understand what wilderness is and what the Congress meant it to be when it created the National Wilderness Preservation System just over 25 years ago. And we must know equally well what wilderness is not: myths about wilderness abound, especially regarding its role in our state's economy.

What is a designated wilderness area?

After decades of effort by concerned citizens from around the country, the Wilderness Act of 1964 was passed by the United States Congress and signed into law. It described wilderness as an area "where the earth and its community of life are untrammeled by man, where man himself is a visitor who does not remain." The Wilderness Act should be seen as the continuation of a great American tradition: conserving some of our most precious and most fragile wild areas. This tradition reaches back to the creation of Yellowstone National Park in 1872 — the first national park to be established anywhere in the world. Despite the existence of national parks, however, it soon became clear that our nation's wild and roadless areas were a rapidly (continued on page 10)

Overleaf: Storm clouds above Mount Nystrom dissolve at day's end, Saint Louis and Vasquez peaks proposed wilderness

THOMAS A. BARRON

INTRODUCTION, CONTINUED

vanishing species, succumbing to the relentless pressures of expanding cities, improved transportation and resource development. Something more was needed, and that something was called designated wilderness.

The Wilderness Act, designed to protect at least a fragment of primeval America for future generations, originally designated 9.1 million acres of federal land as wilderness, including 493,000 acres in Colorado. During the next 15 years, additional acreage was added to the Colorado system. By 1980, the year of Colorado's most recent wilderness legislation, our wilderness lands totalled 2.7 million acres, or 4 percent of the state.

What are the most common myths about wilderness?

Myth Number One: *We already have vast amounts of wilderness in Colorado and don't need any more.* With only 4 percent of Colorado's lands designated as wilderness, this claim is difficult to support. Colorado has 96 percent of its land, and 90 percent of its federal land, in non-wilderness categories. We rank only seventh out of the 11 western states in terms of the acreage currently protected, even though Colorado holds some of the West's most spectacular wild areas. The 20 areas portrayed by John Fielder's photographs in this book would add only an additional 1.3 percent to the state's wilderness total. Is 5 percent of our land too much to set aside for future generations?

Myth Number Two: *Wilderness designation means that lands will be "locked up," making them unavailable for people to use.* On the contrary, people in wilderness areas can hunt, fish, hike, float, canoe, travel on horseback, camp, picnic, cross-country ski, graze livestock and generally do anything else that does not destroy the wilderness character of the land. In order to preserve the unique qualities of wilderness areas, people are not allowed to use motorized equipment, build dams, harvest timber, dig new mines or otherwise alter the original landscape. Wilderness is preserved not only for ourselves; it guarantees that our sons and daughters and their sons and daughters will also be able to know these places. In addition to allowing recreational pursuits, scientific research and protection of clean sources of water, wilderness areas play an important role in our state's economy. They are an irreplaceable part of our heritage, and protecting them ensures they will be available for us all to use and enjoy.

Myth Number Three: *Wilderness costs Colorado jobs and income.* As a businessman, I have little patience with this particular myth, since the facts are clearly otherwise. Recreation and tourism is Colorado's second largest industry, representing $5.6 billion in annual revenues, more than 100,000 direct jobs and many additional, indirect jobs. During the summer of 1989, Colorado hosted 18.5 million visitors who spent $3.5 billion — more than $50 per person per day during the average five-day stay. Of this total, hunting and fishing contributed more than $1.2 billion to the state's economy. Almost one million fishing licenses and 500,000 hunting licenses are sold annually in Colorado, leading to nearly $600 million in spending by hunters and another $687 million by fishermen. Fishermen alone are responsible for generating more than 12,000 jobs in Colorado. Each year, *two million people* visit Colorado's wilderness areas, which is more than 15 percent of total visitations nationally.

These economic facts are especially important in the current debate over the 20 areas highlighted by this book, because so many of the proposed wilderness areas contain important wildlife habitat and prime hunting, fishing and recreation opportunities. Whether or not a particular species may be hunted, protecting its habitat is important for its survival in Colorado. For example, Buffalo Peaks is one of the most productive bighorn sheep areas in the state, providing the only area in Colorado with all the seasonal ranges for a bighorn herd. Fossil Ridge hosts an estimated 800 to 1,200 elk every year for migration and calving. In the Piedra, there are black bear, mountain lion, deer, elk and even river otter, a rare species in Colorado. The Sangre de Cristo Range supports more than 20 major species, including elk, bighorn sheep, black bear, cougar and peregrine falcon. Roubideau is rich in native cutthroat trout, beaver, black bear, deer and golden eagle.

During my years as president of a publicly traded venture capital firm, I learned that a healthy economy and a healthy environment go hand in hand. This principle is especially true of Colorado's remaining wilderness areas, because these lands represent a key competitive advantage for our state. If we harm them, we damage our economic base for the future. If we protect them, we invest in the future.

In addition to creating jobs and bringing revenues from tourism, recreation, hunting and fishing, wilderness means economic value for Colorado because of its role in our state's tradition. We might well call wilderness areas our "scenic ambassadors." No one doubts that most of the visitors to Colorado — visitors who spent $5.6 billion in 1989 — are drawn here by Colorado's distinctive image of pristine mountains, lush alpine meadows and sparkling streams. Similarly, people who bring their families and businesses to this state are attracted by our remarkable heritage of natural areas. The message is clear: if we are to continue to market Colorado successfully in the future, we must preserve some of our finest unspoiled lands.

The value of wilderness cannot be expressed in purely financial terms — much like the value of good health or friends or a strong family. Our willingness to set aside some of our most remarkable places says something about the kind of people we are. But wilderness can also be a significant source of long-term economic strength, if only we are farsighted enough to protect it.

Colorado's magnificent wealth of wilderness is, in business terms, an important part of our capital base. To protect these natural assets is not folly, it is prudent. Our economy's long-term strength depends on these areas remaining intact. To allow them to be developed for some potential short-term gain is analogous to devouring our capital base — and robbing the future.

What lands are being proposed for wilderness, and why are they important?

The 20 areas featured in this book include all but one of the places named in the three Colorado wilderness proposals made recently by members of our congressional delegation. Together they amount to 841,280 acres, using the acreages proposed by Senator Tim Wirth for 18 of the areas, plus the acreages proposed by Representative Ben Nighthorse Campbell for Roubideau and Tabeguache.

A full 252,080 acres, comprising nearly one-third of the lands in question, is included in the proposed Sangre de Cristo wilderness area. This is a land of dramatic contrasts, where towering 14,000-foot peaks rise sharply from the floor of the San Luis

Valley, home to some of Colorado's oldest families, where the Great Sand Dunes are neighbors to snow-fed sparkling streams. Yet another special attribute of the Sangre de Cristo is its proximity to the urban areas of the southern Front Range, providing valuable recreational access to the people of this region.

In addition to the Sangre de Cristo, the 20 proposed wilderness areas include others near the cities of the Front Range. Greenhorn Mountain and Spanish Peaks are also in the southern part of the state. Williams Fork (near the Eisenhower Tunnel), Saint Louis and Vasquez peaks (not far from Berthoud Pass) and Buffalo Peaks (close to South Park) are readily accessible to the bulk of Colorado's population. The American Flats area and the Williams Fork area both provide unusual opportunities for access by the elderly and the physically disabled, making them valuable additions to Colorado's wilderness system.

Approximately 131,000 acres of this total are proposed additions — lands adjacent to existing wilderness areas. They are integral pieces of the wilderness ecosystems that were not included in the original designations. These areas would help to complete each wilderness unit in terms of wildlife habitat, biological diversity and aesthetic integrity. They include Davis Peak, Lost Creek addition, Oh! Be Joyful, South San Juan additions, Spruce Creek, Weminuche additions, Wheeler Geologic and the lands adjacent to the Big Blue Wilderness: Bill Hare Gulch, Larson Creek and American Flats.

Another group of proposed areas would add significant lower-elevation forests to the wilderness system in Colorado. Forests of this type are now largely absent from our wilderness lands. The Piedra, Service Creek, Buffalo Peaks, Roubideau and Tabeguache areas contain pristine forests and streams under 10,000 feet in elevation. Heavily forested canyons like Roubideau and Tabeguache are very important to the ecological integrity of their regions, and are increasingly rare in Colorado.

Each of the proposed areas represents a significant contribution to our wilderness heritage. Cannibal Plateau (named in honor of Alferd Packer, its most famous visitor) comprises the largest continuous expanse of tundra in the lower 48 states. Oh! Be Joyful is so spectacular that the residents of nearby Crested Butte have, in the words of Representative Campbell, "*demanded* that it be included" in any wilderness legislation, despite the loss of use of their motorized vehicles that would result. Service Creek, south of Rabbit Ears Pass, and Piedra, in the San Juan Mountains, hold some of the last virgin spruce and fir forests left in Colorado.

The clock is ticking for all of these areas, as development pressure intensifies. The Forest Service estimates that in the Sangre de Cristo area alone, at least 20,000 acres have lost their wilderness qualities during the past few years as the wilderness debate has dragged on.

How do the three Colorado wilderness proposals differ from one another?

There are major differences among the three wilderness proposals made during the past year by members of Colorado's congressional delegation. Senator Wirth, Senator Bill Armstrong and Representative Campbell have each offered proposals with divergent philosophies, acreage amounts and attitudes toward wilderness water.

Senator Wirth's bill seeks to protect 751,260 acres, including 252,080 acres in the Sangre de Cristo area, but excluding the 60,000-acre Piedra, which remains in wilderness study status. His underlying philosophy is that wilderness is important for Colorado's economic health and quality of life, now and in the future. His bill takes into careful consideration the boundaries of affected ecosystems in each region. The Wirth bill would give wilderness areas a federal water right that would be adjudicated in Colorado water court under Colorado law, guaranteeing them a sufficient quantity of water to preserve wilderness values.

By contrast, Senator Armstrong's bill would protect 471,875 acres, including 195,100 acres in the Sangre de Cristo area. His underlying philosophy is that traditional forms of economic development always take precedence, regardless of their potentially damaging effects on the long-term economic health and environmental quality of a particular region. His bill would prohibit a federal water right and would leave no guarantee that wilderness areas would be able to retain enough water to protect their wilderness qualities. The Armstrong bill would require the federal government to ask the Colorado Water Conservation Board, a state water development agency, to file for a minimum streamflow under Colorado water law.

Representative Campbell's proposal includes 641,410 acres of wilderness, which includes Roubideau and Tabeguache, two areas not mentioned in the Wirth bill but excludes the 41,500-acre Piedra which remains in wilderness study status. His proposal, like Senator Wirth's, would provide a federal water right to wilderness, although with a much lower quantification standard, preserving only enough water so that the primary purpose of wilderness would not be entirely defeated. This water right, like Senator Wirth's, would be adjudicated in Colorado water court.

We in Colorado are blessed with an extraordinary array of wilderness lands. The question before us now is whether we have the wisdom to keep some of them, for ourselves and for the generations that follow. Whether or not we are fortunate enough to visit all of the places featured in this book, we can always benefit from the peace of mind that comes from knowing that they are there. If these lands can be protected, unspoiled and intact, it will lift our spirits just to know that we can explore them any time we choose.

Wilderness provides Coloradans with the means to make a living as well as the chance to have a life worth living. The Greek word *ecos* is the root of both of our words *economy* and *ecology*, reminding us that keeping our economy in business over the long term means keeping our environment healthy. The bottom line is this: the opposite of conservation is destruction, the opposite of preservation is waste.

I, for one, hope that my grandchildren will have the same opportunity that I have had to sit on a rock by an alpine stream, spy a paw print in the wet earth and wonder . . . might it be a mountain lion?

— THOMAS A. BARRON

DAVIS PEAK (MOUNT ZIRKEL ADDITION)

Size: 36,000 acres
Elevation: 8,600 to 11,100 feet
Flora: Engelmann spruce, subalpine fir, lodgepole pine, alpine tundra, meadow
Fauna: Elk, deer, black bear, pine marten, wolverine, trout
Uncommon species: None
Routt National Forest

There are fishermen who approach trout streams on their bellies, squirming to the edge of a favorite pool, hoping to keep a stray shadow from warning wily trout of their presence. Such fishermen are drawn to the Encampment River, a wilderness waterway in northwestern Colorado. Beginning as trickles of snowmelt high in the Park Range and the Sierra Madre, the Encampment takes life as larger and larger rivulets coalesce from gravity tugging them downhill toward Wyoming. The river winds through luxuriant meadows as it flows north, creating a series of pools and riffles that provides ideal habitat for trout. The pristine condition of this wilderness river led the Forest Service to recommend it for federal protection under the Wild and Scenic Rivers Act, a recommendation Congress has yet to act upon.

The river's headwaters originate within the Mount Zirkel Wilderness, but the wilderness boundary was inexplicably drawn to exclude the more biologically productive downstream reaches of the river. Black Mountain, a thumb thrust between the Main and West forks of the Encampment, defines the current wilderness boundary. The Davis Peak Further Planning Area straddles both forks of the Encampment, draped around Black Mountain and the northern edge of the Mount Zirkel Wilderness like a

wilderness shawl. Six miles of each fork of the Encampment are included in the roadless area.

Mount Zirkel was one of Colorado's five original wilderness areas, designated in the Wilderness Act of 1964. The area was enlarged considerably in 1980 Colorado wilderness legislation, when significant forested tracts were added south of Mount Zirkel. The area's northern boundaries received less attention. However, the Davis Peak addition corrects this oversight by extending the range of life zones included in the wilderness to those in the biologically rich lower elevations of the Encampment River.

The subdued foothills of the Park Range comprise the eastern extent of the Davis Peak roadless area, with low, rolling, forested ridges interspersed with sprawling meadows. Though the Continental Divide traverses the western end of Davis Peak as it exits Colorado en route to the lower elevations of southern Wyoming, the divide has greatly mellowed from its more common skyscraping Colorado heights. Davis Peak is truly a bridge between the rugged peaks of the Mount Zirkel Wilderness — the most northern example of rock-and-ice Colorado wilderness — and more sedate lowland forests.

Above: Fallen tree pierces mirror-smooth waters of upper Big Creek Lake   Right: Water lilies decorate one
of many kettle ponds left by receding glaciers   Overleaf: Lily pads float on azure waters of a large kettle pond

SERVICE CREEK

Size: 54,700 acres
Elevation: 7,000 to 10,700 feet
Flora: Lodgepole pine, Engelmann spruce, subalpine fir, aspen, grassland, sagebrush
Fauna: Elk, deer, black bear, mountain lion, trout
Uncommon species: None
Routt National Forest

Service Creek is to Colorado's northern forests what the Piedra roadless area is to the state's southern forests — an absolutely pristine enclave of magnificent forested wildlands. Located south of Rabbit Ears Pass in the southern end of the Park Range, Service Creek is one of the last significant tracts of undeveloped forest in Colorado. The area was overlooked in previous wilderness legislation because of interest in it from timber companies and simply because it lacks the spectacular alpine features of more typical Colorado wilderness.

Two large creeks, Service and Silver, beckon as they exit the rolling forests that flank the open valley of the Yampa River. When a hiker enters these primeval forests, crowds are quickly exchanged for the protective, closed environs of the sheltering trees. The creeks meander through the forest, ducking under fallen logs, skirting gravel bars, providing cover for the darting shadows of trout, and bending to and fro in a relentless journey to the Yampa. Now and then the forest cover breaks to reveal meadows that squish underfoot with every step.

Service Creek was actually named *Sarvis* Creek by locals. A misinformed or misdirected mapmaker changed the written name to *Service*, perhaps in reference to the serviceberry bush.

Current wilderness legislation hopes to correct history and restore the original Sarvis Creek moniker.

Progress marches inexorably onward, and in Colorado it often takes the form of massive new ski areas. Steamboat Ski Corporation is planning a giant ski resort, Lake Catamount, for the edge of Service Creek. For some inscrutable reason, the Forest Service has joined forces with the developer and now advocates stripping several thousand acres from lands it just recently proposed for wilderness. Several ski runs would be cut in the Green Creek drainage, shrinking an already-too-small remnant of virgin wildlands.

The timber industry has also made loud noises opposing wilderness designation of Service Creek, despite the minuscule amount of timber that could be harvested and the substantial taxpayer subsidy that such harvesting would require. Hallmarks of modern civilization, including ski areas and logging, are ever expanding into previously unmarked country. It is a race between the fading gasps of traditional resource development and an awakening environmental consciousness that manifests itself through protection of vanishing wilderness.

Above: Dense forests of fir, spruce, pine and aspen reclaim old beaver ponds
Right: Rock outcropping overlooks vast tracts of undeveloped forest

SAINT LOUIS AND VASQUEZ PEAKS

Size: 24,200 acres
Elevation: 8,600 to 12,800 feet
Flora: Tundra, Engelmann spruce, subalpine fir, lodgepole pine
Fauna: Elk, deer, black bear, mountain goat, pine marten, golden eagle
Uncommon species: None
Arapaho National Forest

A narrow neck of windswept tundra connects the Vasquez Peak Wilderness Study Area and the Saint Louis Peak Further Planning Area. Although two distinct administrative units, the areas are in fact one contiguous stretch of high-country wilderness. The areas form a rough half-moon, following the sweep of the Vasquez Mountains from Berthoud Pass to Byers Peak. The pinched waist of the area belies its remoteness: the southern boundary is nothing but a power-line corridor, while the northern boundary is an undeveloped tract of the Fraser Experimental Forest.

This roadless area offers an unparalleled opportunity to partake of a uniquely Colorado recreational pursuit, namely a miles-long stroll above treeline with nothing but eagles and clouds to obstruct the scenery. Beginning at Berthoud Pass, a hiker need never duck below treeline until reaching the far end of the range near Bottle Peak, some 20 miles distant. There is something positively sinful about such unfettered enjoyment of Colorado's mountain riches.

More and more Coloradans are immersing themselves in these mountain riches every year. Visits to Colorado wilderness areas have grown by more than 200 percent since 1977. Other popular back-country areas near the heavily populated Front Range, including the Indian Peaks Wilderness and Rocky Mountain National Park, have instituted permit systems whereby the numbers of hikers and other recreationists are restricted to prevent fragile high country from being loved to death. Areas such as Saint Louis and Vasquez peaks offer a positive alternative to permit systems by preserving equally spectacular, if lesser known, wildlands in close proximity to 1.5 million people. Year after year, the value of these wildlands for recreational and scenic retreats increases immeasurably.

Above: Alpine grasses float on still waters of a tundra pool
Right: Rock talus decorates ridges high above treeline

WILLIAMS FORK

Size: 40,000 acres
Elevation: 8,800 to 13,500 feet
Flora: Alpine tundra, Engelmann spruce, subalpine fir, lodgepole pine
Fauna: Elk, deer, black bear, blue grouse, trout
Uncommon species: None
Arapaho National Forest

In summer, a hiker can park at the Eisenhower Tunnel, strap on a pack, skirt the whining tunnel exhausts and climb steeply to the Continental Divide. From here, the roar and fumes of Interstate 70 fade, and a spectacular display of alpine wildflowers beckons. Following the divide north to Hagar Mountain, the Williams Fork basin opens beneath the feet, drawing the eye and soul into an as yet unspoiled wilderness.

Williams Fork bridges the often-yawning gap between the commotion of modern civilization and the serenity of wilderness. Its southern boundary is I-70 and one of man's mightiest monuments to the conquest of nature, the Eisenhower Tunnel. The Williams Fork Mountains shield the bulk of the area from the influence of the highway so that proximity to I-70 means easy escape from the bedlam of Denver and reminds visitors to Williams Fork of the value of wild sanctuaries.

The forks of the Williams Fork River are easily circumnavigated following a trail that loops through the center of the area. Rich wetlands — formed by creeks that pool and pond — fill broad glacial valleys and create ideal habitat for trout, beaver and other riparian creatures. This same lush wetness, combined with nearness to Denver, has unfortunately made Williams Fork a principal battleground in the continuing water wars between the Eastern and Western slopes of Colorado.

The Denver Water Board wants to divert 42,000 acre-feet of water annually through a system of high-altitude canals and pipelines. Senator Wirth's bill eliminates the Denver Water Board desired acreage. The Water Board's gravity-fed system would mean extensive cut-and-fill construction following elevation contours and would result in blatant linear scars across 36 miles of unroaded forest. An example of this proposed scenario is readily apparent along Bobtail Creek. A more benign assault on Williams Fork water proposes a small reservoir farther down the valley, with water pumped to the Front Range in a less intrusive pipeline.

As with the adjacent Saint Louis and Vasquez peaks roadless area, Williams Fork is ideally situated to relieve recreational pressure on existing Front Range wilderness. Access to the Williams Fork back country from the Eisenhower Tunnel or via Herman Gulch is but a short hour's drive up I-70 from Denver. Many might consider it unexpected good fortune to have a prime wilderness astride the state's main vehicular thoroughfare, just outside the state's largest urban center. Certainly such a wilderness is too precious to sacrifice to unnecessarily damaging water development schemes when competitive alternatives exist.

Above: Alpine ridges reflect in a tarn below Coon Hill
Right: Evening light colors the Continental Divide and a pool of snowmelt

Above: Fir snag reflects a blue morning sky below 13,553-foot Pettingell Peak
Right: Abstract patterns in morning light

LOST CREEK ADDITION

Size: 11,000 acres
Elevation: 8,500 to 12,300 feet
Flora: Alpine vegetation, krummholz, spruce/fir, lodgepole pine, aspen
Fauna: Elk, deer, bighorn sheep
Uncommon species: None
Pike National Forest

It might be easy to lose the Lost Creek wilderness addition among the crush of other areas. The current 106,000-acre Lost Creek Wilderness was designated by Congress in 1980 to protect the rugged back country of the Tarryall, Platte River and Kenosha mountains. As Congress wound down in 1980, it found it lacked the necessary information to complete the northwestern boundary of the Lost Creek Wilderness. Out of this was born the Lost Creek Further Planning Area.

The Lost Creek addition consists of 11,000 acres just south of Kenosha Pass. North and South Twin Cone peaks, the northern end of the Platte River mountains, form the core of the area. Moist meadows are scattered amid the forested slopes of the peaks. The Ben Tyler Trail slices to the heart of the wilderness addition, ultimately crossing the watershed divide and descending into Rock Creek.

What could be controversial about so small a wilderness addition? It turns out, not much. The 11,000-acre addition was carved out of a larger 23,000-acre unit and was whittled to its present size through the deletion of old logging roads, radio transmitters and the like. It was precisely because of questions about the location of these obvious non-wilderness features that Congress left the area for further study.

Designating the addition as wilderness would complete protection for the Platte River mountains. Bighorn sheep lambing areas along Rock Creek would be incorporated into the wilderness, and a popular recreational trail would gain the added recognition and protection of wilderness. With this addition, Lost Creek would increase its role as a welcome wilderness retreat for Front Range residents.

Above: Rime ice left by a retreating early-season storm, flanks of Mount Blaine
Right: Rock forms imitate cloud shapes in evening light, flanks of Mount Blaine

SPRUCE CREEK (HUNTER–FRYINGPAN ADDITION)

Size: 8,000 acres
Elevation: 9,200 to 12,200 feet
Flora: Spruce/fir, aspen, meadow, riparian
Fauna: Elk, deer, mountain lion, pine marten, lynx, wolverine
Uncommon species: Cutthroat trout
White River National Forest

Encompassing the dramatic mountain scenery north of Independence Pass is the Hunter–Fryingpan Wilderness, so designated by Congress in 1976 as part of the Endangered American Wilderness Act. But a pie-shaped wedge of land along Spruce Creek, a forested portal into the land above treeline, was left out of the wilderness because of logging interest in its lush forests of spruce and fir. This small area has been in wilderness limbo ever since, although the logging companies that originally objected to wilderness designation have long since left the region.

Spruce Creek is a delightful backyard getaway from the summer tourist crush that descends upon neighboring Aspen. Drawn to the dramatic peaks and valleys of the Elk Mountains, Aspen visitors often overlook shadowy retreats such as Spruce Creek. The headwaters of the creek are in a forest meadow below the high peaks of the Elks, which beckon on the horizon. The creek flows across lazy fields of wildflowers, gradually gaining speed as it tumbles past moss-covered forest behemoths and doubling in volume with the capture of a tributary. Spruce Creek is a place of sounds — the rush of wind through the treetops, the gurgle and splash of the creek, the silent blanket of the deep forest.

Above: Lush forests of spruce and fir, confluence of Woody and Spruce creeks
Right: Woody Creek takes a plunge on its way to the Roaring Fork River

BUFFALO PEAKS

Size: 58,200 acres
Elevation: 9,200 to 13,326 feet
Flora: Engelmann spruce, Douglas fir, aspen, ponderosa pine, piñon/juniper, meadow, alpine vegetation
Fauna: Pine marten, bighorn sheep, elk, deer, northern three-toed woodpecker, trout
Uncommon species: None
Pike and San Isabel national forests

A breeze whispers, Colorado's famous aspen quiver as befits their "quakies" nickname, and a huge elk abruptly raises its massive rack to peer at the hiker who has intruded into this meadow sanctuary. Few would suspect that this gentle valley in the heart of the Buffalo Peaks roadless area is but a stone's throw from the highest range in Colorado — the mighty Collegiates. Four of Colorado's five tallest peaks loom on the horizon, across the Arkansas River valley from the mild mountain afterthought that is the Buffalo Peaks. Buffalo Peaks offers a geographic and recreational alternative to the imposing beauty of the Collegiates and their rocky, windswept summits that descend steeply into deep, U-shaped valleys.

The Buffalo Peaks themselves are gentle talus mounds rising above the southern end of the roadless area. While the peaks are a distinct feature, they by no means dominate the large timbered basins, pure mountain streams and expansive subalpine meadows that surround them. Buffalo Peaks draws the visitor who seeks the solitude of a forest, the panorama of the mighty Collegiates, the relaxation of an undisturbed stroll through meadows and past big game. One scenic trail loops into Buffalo Meadows, heads up Rich Creek and returns via Rough and Tumbling Creek.

Those in search of more rugged explorations can pursue the route to a natural arch, uncommon in the forests of the central Rockies, below Marmot Peak. With luck they may glimpse the local bighorn sheep, which find both winter and summer range within the bounds of the proposed wilderness.

Buffalo Peaks lies within easy driving distance of the Denver metropolitan area and other Front Range population centers. The gentle nature of the area and its diverse recreational opportunities argue strongly for wilderness protection. The ease of access, however, allows civilization to continue its unchecked advance. Firewood cutting, radio transmitters and the Homestake water pipeline define the boundaries of Buffalo Peaks. Aurora and Colorado Springs want to construct yet another water pipeline a few short miles north of the existing one, eating up thousands of acres of prime wilderness in the process. Others clamor for more firewood, more TV transmitters, more access to elusive mineral claims and newly opened livestock grazing ranges. The resolution of these competing demands will define the extent, or perhaps even the existence, of the Buffalo Peaks Wilderness.

Above: Evening moon reflects in a small pond near Weston Pass, with Buffalo Peaks in the distance
Right: Early morning light on West Buffalo Peak

OH! BE JOYFUL (RAGGEDS ADDITION)

Size: 5,500 acres
Elevation: 9,500 to 12,700 feet
Flora: Engelmann spruce, subalpine fir, alpine tundra
Fauna: Elk, deer, black bear, trout
Uncommon species: *Leucorrhinia hudsonica* (a dragonfly)
Gunnison National Forest

Oh! Be Joyful! Few other names capture the joy of wilderness so succinctly. Oh! Be Joyful is 5,500 acres packed full of glacial creations — hanging valleys, cirques, tarns, arêtes, horns and majestic U-shaped valleys. Its dramatic appearance is further heightened by striking bands of rock along valley walls and cliffs.

While Oh! Be Joyful stirs the hearts of wilderness lovers, it has been shrouded with controversy. An extension of the existing Raggeds Wilderness near Crested Butte, Oh! Be Joyful has the misfortune to lie only a mile from the Mount Emmons molybdenum deposit, an ore body that AMAX proposed to develop as part of a giant mine complex in 1980. This proximity has stymied efforts at wilderness designation, as mining and wilderness proponents have locked horns. Congress requested further study for Oh! Be Joyful in 1980 Colorado wilderness legislation, in order to more carefully weigh its outstanding wilderness value against potential mineral development.

The Raggeds are a modest, though rough (hence the name), range running from Crested Butte to Marble. A north-south ridge, the Ruby Range, forms the current eastern boundary of the wilderness. To the west of the Ruby Range, the Raggeds Wilderness drains the watershed of Anthracite Creek. Oh! Be Joyful adds an eastern entrance to the wilderness, providing a beautiful passage up the Oh! Be Joyful Valley to Oh! Be Joyful Pass, a gateway through the Ruby Range into the adjacent wilderness.

While the unsurpassed beauty of Oh! Be Joyful is reason enough to ensure its protection through wilderness designation, the area is also highly prized by the town of Crested Butte for its pure water. Crested Butte has identified the valley as its secondary source for municipal water.

Above: Alpine asters bloom below Daisy Pass   Right: Oh! Be Joyful Peak reflects joy onto a small pond

Above: As lush an alpine valley as there ever was, below Peele Peak
Right: Indian paintbrush wildflowers below Oh! Be Joyful Peak

FOSSIL RIDGE

Size: 55,600 acres
Elevation: 8,500 to 13,200 feet
Flora: Spruce/fir, lodgepole pine, aspen, meadow, alpine tundra
Fauna: Elk, deer, mountain goat, black bear, mountain lion, bobcat, pine marten, trout
Uncommon species: Sculler's willow, *Braya humilis* (mustard family)
Gunnison National Forest

At one time, Fossil Ridge rated among the most pristine wilderness candidates in Colorado. Under the Forest Service's subjective ranking system for evaluating potential wilderness areas, Fossil Ridge's score of 25 out of 28 possible points placed it among the elite of virgin wildlands. Unfortunately, resource management of Fossil Ridge has been lackadaisical at best, and this pristine wilderness gem is now in imminent danger of falling under the mechanized wheels of civilization.

At the heart of Gunnison County, Fossil Ridge is by anyone's estimation an absolutely magical wilderness kingdom. Lofty ridges snake through the area, among them Fossil Ridge, so named for its fossil-bearing limestone beds which reveal sea fossils raised more than two miles above sea level. From one of these ridges, surrounded by many of Colorado's mightiest ranges, hikers can pick out 22 of the state's 54 peaks over 14,000 feet. The high ridges are shared with a small herd of mountain goats which has migrated from the nearby Collegiate Peaks.

One of seven alpine fishing lakes is often the focal point of a visit to Fossil Ridge. In an abrupt transition, geology in the area changes from limestone beds to granite bedrock. Consequently, lakes on one side of Fossil Ridge are highly alkaline, while lakes only two miles distant, situated on granite, are quite sensitive to acids. This dichotomy in water chemistry provides a marvelous opportunity to evaluate the impact of acid precipitation on high-altitude lakes.

Wildlife experts have estimated that upwards of 1,000 elk use Fossil Ridge for at least some part of their lives. Not unexpectedly, several big-game outfitters thrive on the business generated by sportsmen who each fall escape the rigors of civilization to pursue a more intimate relationship with the earth.

The silence of Fossil Ridge has been split in recent years by ever-increasing numbers of motorcycles and other off-highway vehicles. Surprisingly, the Forest Service has interpreted Congress' direction — to protect the wilderness character of study areas such as Fossil Ridge — as permission to advocate motorized use of the area, a use in direct conflict with wilderness. Signs encouraging motor vehicles to embark into the wilderness study area have been placed by the Forest Service at major trailheads. This official disregard for the wilderness values of Fossil Ridge has led to strident arguments between motorists and wilderness supporters. The "trammeling" of Fossil Ridge is one of the motivating factors behind the need for additional wilderness areas, lands that are by definition maintained in an untrammeled condition for future generations.

Above: Aspen leaves cover the trail to Lamphier Lakes   Right: Thin crust of ice reflects a peak above upper Lamphier Lake   Overleaf: Ridges above upper Lamphier Lake catch the first light of morning

ROUBIDEAU

Size: 19,800 acres (Campbell)
Elevation: 5,600 to 9,600 feet
Flora: Spruce/fir, aspen, ponderosa, oak brush, piñon/juniper
Fauna: Elk, deer, black bear, bobcat, cougar, golden eagle, cutthroat trout, beaver
Uncommon species: None
Uncompahgre National Forest

The Uncompahgre Plateau is a hundred-mile-long uplift that begins in dramatic fashion in the red rock canyons of Colorado National Monument outside of Grand Junction and ends in a surge against the flanks of the Sneffels Range. The plateau spans a range of ecosystems from the driest desert canyons to the lushest spruce/fir and aspen forests. It is an unparalleled landform with ecological diversity that is exceeded few other places in Colorado. Yet not a single acre of the plateau has been offered any protection from modern civilization to ensure the preservation of some fragment of this unique environment for future enjoyment and study.

What makes the Uncompahgre Plateau such a magnificent ecological storehouse also contributes to its ready development. Since the late 1800s its broad slopes have been easily invaded by roads for cattle grazing and logging. The only substantial unroaded segments of the Uncompahgre are several canyons whose steep walls have thus far precluded extensive development. Roubideau is the longest remaining roadless canyon, stretching 20 miles from its source in Uncompahgre National Forest to the bleak Gunnison River desert near Delta.

Named for French fur trapper Antoine Robidoux, the canyon originates in subalpine spruce and aspen forests. As it flows northward, Roubideau Creek cuts into the Mesozoic sandstone that is draped over the dome of the Uncompahgre uplift. Dakota, Morrison, Entrada and Chinle strata form cliffs of warm colors that frame a lush riparian ecosystem in the canyon bottom. The creek traverses several life zones, leaving the aspen/spruce forests for ponderosa pine and oak brush, and, ultimately, the dry reaches of the lower canyon populated by intermittent cottonwoods. Roubideau is a wide and leisurely canyon. It follows the grade of the plateau and maintains a uniform depth from its source to its mouth. The canyon slopes seem to have tired of their roles; many slumps are apparent where the overlying Morrison has drooped in great sheets across brilliant red, orange and white bands of Entrada sandstone.

Perhaps Roubideau Canyon has maintained its wildness because of the accessibility of the surrounding mesas. But the pace of logging has increased in recent years. Numerous new logging roads have punched to the edges of the canyon — so many they no longer appear on official road maps. Recent plans of Uncompahgre National Forest officials propose invasion of the southeastern slopes of the canyon for access to its virgin timber.

Above: Roubideau Creek framed by a lush riparian ecosystem
Right: Spring colors decorate the banks of Roubideau Creek

TABEGUACHE

Size: 10,300 acres (Campbell)
Elevation: 6,000 to 9,700 feet
Flora: Spruce/fir, aspen, ponderosa, oak brush, piñon/juniper
Fauna: Elk, deer, bobcat, cougar, black bear, trout
Uncommon species: None
Uncompahgre National Forest

Tabeguache Creek and its North Fork begin in fertile subalpine bowls atop the Uncompahgre Plateau. Tabeguache Creek plunges quickly into a steep-walled canyon of brilliant red sandstone. The North Fork takes a more leisurely route, winding through an unbroken expanse of vibrant aspen before it, too, drops abruptly into a deep canyon lined by red sandstone cliffs. The red cliffs, normally associated with desert terrains, seem somehow out of place surrounded by the lush greenery of this unique melding of canyon and mountain country.

Tabeguache is named for the Tabeguache band of Utes who roamed the Uncompahgre Plateau until 1880, when they were exiled to the Uintah Reservation in Utah. The word *Tabeguache* loosely translates as "Place Where the Snows Melt First" or "Sunny Side." True to its name, Tabeguache Creek drains the southwestern escarpment of the Uncompahgre Plateau. The plateau is a broad shield that rises gradually from the east to a deceptive elevation more than a mile above its surrounding plains. Upon reaching its crest, the wave of the plateau breaks. The western drainages, such as Tabeguache, cut sharply into the broken wave in a rough-and-tumble hurry to the San Miguel and Dolores rivers.

In the heart of Tabeguache Canyon, the serenity of the higher aspen forests is quickly forgotten. Here, Father Time keeps a stable of stately ponderosa pine giants whose toes are swept by the unruly whitewater leaps of Tabeguache Creek during its wild spring runoff. The towering ponderosas are themselves dwarfed by the rising red cliffs of Wingate sandstone. Oak brush and other common shrubs cling to the broken slopes of the canyon, eventually yielding to the white-barked aspen forests of the upper slopes.

These aspen forests stir the heart of not only the curious observer, but also the timber baron. Several aspen clear-cuts have crept into the edges of the Tabeguache roadless area to fuel the corporate engines of the Louisiana-Pacific waferwood mill in nearby Olathe. A combination of aspen clear-cuts from the north and ponderosa pine harvests from east and west creates an ever-tightening vise of development around Tabeguache.

There is extensive evidence of early occupation of Tabeguache Canyon by ancient civilizations. An early archeological excavation of Tabeguache Cave provided artifacts from the Archaic period perhaps as long ago as 2000 B.C. and from more recent historic Ute cultures.

Above: Red sandstone cliffs of the Uncompahgre Plateau
Right: Rugged, terraced walls of Tabeguache Canyon

CANNIBAL PLATEAU–POWDERHORN

Size: 70,000 acres
Elevation: 8,800 to 12,644 feet
Flora: Alpine tundra, spruce/fir, aspen, ponderosa pine, sagebrush
Fauna: Elk, deer, bighorn sheep, black bear, mountain lion, trout
Uncommon species: None
Gunnison National Forest

In the winter of 1874, a group of six men followed the Lake Fork of the Gunnison to a point where it veers west to its headwaters in the San Juan Mountains. Perhaps realizing their error in direction or perhaps because of heavy snows, the group stopped at the foot of a broad alpine plateau. Only one of the group, Alferd Packer, was ever heard from again, and his tale gained him notoriety as Colorado's most famous cannibal.

In honor or remembrance of Alferd Packer's aberrant behavior, the alpine plateau was christened Cannibal Plateau. Together with neighboring Calf Creek Plateau, Cannibal Plateau forms one of the largest and least disturbed expanses of alpine tundra in the country. Few other areas in Colorado give rise to an equivalent sense of vastness, for its 12,000-foot elevation affords unrestricted views of the San Juan, Elk and Sawatch ranges. Literally thousands of acres of rolling tundra are broken by an occasional broad valley or clear blue lake populated with brook and brown trout.

The majority of the Cannibal Plateau roadless area is actually administered not by the Forest Service, but by the Bureau of Land Management. The BLM's Powderhorn Primitive Area com-prises approximately two-thirds of the roadless acreage. Powderhorn Primitive Area was formally designated by the secretary of Interior in 1973. At the time, the Wilderness Act did not extend to include lands administered by the BLM. It was not until the passage of the Federal Land Policy and Management Act in 1976 that BLM lands were folded into the protective umbrella of wilderness. The BLM moved soon thereafter to propose Powderhorn for official wilderness designation. Upon this desig-nation, Powderhorn would become the first BLM wilderness area in Colorado.

The Forest Service–BLM boundary arbitrarily splits the Cannibal and Calf Creek plateaus along an imaginary straight line that crosses from east to west on undifferentiated tundra. In 1980, Congress postponed consideration of wilderness designation for the Forest Service's Cannibal Plateau area pending the BLM's wilderness recommendation for the adjacent Powderhorn Primi-tive Area. A favorable proposal has been received from the BLM, and the time has come to permanently preserve a most fragile alpine treasure.

Above: Powderhorn Lakes are the nexus of this vast alpine plateau above Powderhorn Lakes

Right: Morning light colors talus slopes
Overleaf: Last night's storm makes great fodder for patterns of the new day

BIG BLUE ADDITIONS

Size: 3,900 acres
Elevation: 8,600 to 13,000 feet
Flora: Alpine tundra, ponderosa pine, Engelmann spruce, subalpine fir
Fauna: Elk, deer, bighorn sheep, blue grouse
Uncommon species: Altai starwort and Porter's groundsel
Adjacent to Uncompahgre National Forest (BLM Gunnison Basin Resource Area)

Southwestern Colorado's Uncompahgre Range is perhaps the state's most photogenic. Courthouse Mountain, glacier-carved horns such as Wetterhorn and Matterhorn, massive Uncompahgre Peak and Pinnacle Ridge form a spectacular backdrop to Ouray, the self-proclaimed "Switzerland of America." In recognition of this remarkable beauty, Congress set aside most of the Uncompahgre mountains as the Big Blue Wilderness in 1980. The wilderness stopped at the boundary of Uncompahgre National Forest. Equally magnificent alpine country adjacent to the Big Blue Wilderness, but under the administration of the Bureau of Land Management (Department of Interior) instead of the Forest Service (Department of Agriculture), was left unprotected.

The most significant of these wilderness omissions was American Flats, the watershed divide that separates Cow Creek and Wildhorse Creek from Henson Creek. Cow Creek, draining northward toward Ouray, is considered by many local residents to be one of the most rugged and wild drainages in all of the San Juan Mountains. The current wilderness boundary lops the head of the watershed from its body; including American Flats in the Big Blue Wilderness would remedy this situation.

The southerly drainages of American Flats offer welcome relief to the rigor of Cow Creek. The aptly named flats are gentle, slightly undulating hills far above treeline. From them protrudes imposing Wildhorse Peak. American Lake, a small tarn perched on the hillside above Henson Creek, is the source of one branch of the creek. Henson Creek provides municipal water to the town of Lake City, emphasizing the value of undisturbed wilderness as protection for high-quality water supplies.

The Engineer Pass road forms the southern boundary of American Flats and is a popular summertime touring route. For those who bounce along in oblivion, failing to peer over the slight road cut, the grandeur of American Flats is missed even though access to the tundra is easily gained.

American Flats is the largest of three additions to the Big Blue Wilderness. Bill Hare Gulch and Larson Creek, at the opposite end of the ecological spectrum from American Flats, lie a few miles north of Lake City on the edges of the wilderness in the Lake Fork of the Gunnison River valley. Whereas American Flats is treeless, these two areas include low-elevation ponderosa pine and spruce/fir forests that provide crucial deer and elk winter range. Bill Hare Gulch additionally offers the potential for trail access to the Big Blue Wilderness through an area presently blocked by private land.

Above: Tundra at American Flats precedes peaks of the San Juan Mountains
Right: Henson Creek irrigates fields of fireweed wildflowers

Above: Double rainbow over American Flats   Right: Morning light colors the tundra below Wildhorse Peak

WHEELER GEOLOGIC (LA GARITA ADDITION)

Size: 25,000 acres
Elevation: 8,800 to 12,880 feet
Flora: Spruce/fir, aspen, subalpine park
Fauna: Elk, deer, bighorn sheep, black bear, bobcat, blue grouse, trout
Uncommon species: None
Rio Grande National Forest

Deep in the San Juan Mountains, nestled against the very spine of La Garita Range, is a place of mysterious rock spires. The erosive forces of wind, water and ice have carved volcanic tuff into an intriguing array of multicolored caves, domes, pinnacles and fluted walls. These "sand stones," so named by the Utes, form the Wheeler Geologic Study Area.

Wheeler gained early recognition for its unusual rock formations. In 1908, President Theodore Roosevelt proclaimed it a national monument. Wheeler failed to live up to its billing as a tourist-oriented monument, however, owing to its extremely remote location and difficult access, and Congress revoked the national monument designation in 1950. Conservationists have been working to assure protection of Wheeler's wilderness character ever since.

Wheeler covers the southern slopes of La Garita Range. Adjacent La Garita Wilderness was among Colorado's first, designated by Congress in 1964 as part of the original Wilderness Act. La Garita Wilderness was defined to include only lands from La Garita divide to the north, however, and none of the lush forests and rich wildlife habitat to the south. As an addition to La Garita, Wheeler would finally be accorded needed wilderness protection.

Exotic rock formations are only a tiny piece of the pristine wildlands that comprise the Wheeler Geologic Study Area. Perhaps the most significant remaining stands of virgin spruce and fir forest in the Rio Grande basin exist in two magnificent parks, Wasson and Silver. The old-growth timber in these areas is more than 250 years old and has yet to feel the hand of man. These virgin forests and their undisturbed habitat for big-game herds would greatly extend the ecological diversity protected as wilderness in La Garita Range.

Above: Thirty-foot-high "coneheads" of eroded volcanic ash   Right: Balancing rock eroded by the forces of
wind, water and ice   Overleaf: Evening light bathes formations on the edge of La Garita Wilderness

SANGRE DE CRISTO

Size: 252,000 acres
Elevation: 8,200 to 14,345 feet
Flora: Spruce/fir, Douglas fir, ponderosa pine, alpine tundra
Fauna: Bighorn sheep, elk, deer, pine marten, goshawk, northern three-toed woodpecker, cutthroat trout, black bear, cougar, peregrine falcon   Uncommon species: Greenback cutthroat trout
San Isabel and Rio Grande national forests

Lofty crags, massive peaks, cascading waterfalls, hidden alpine lakes — these make the Sangre de Cristos one of Colorado's truly magnificent mountain ranges. Faulting has thrust Precambrian granites and sediments thousands of feet above the surrounding San Luis and Wet Mountain valleys and has created the barrier that traps the windblown detritus of the Great Sand Dunes. Seven 14,000-foot peaks straddle the divide of the Sangres, keeping company with more than 30 other peaks above 13,000 feet. The Sangre de Cristo peaks are among Colorado's most rugged, their names synonymous with epic feats of Colorado mountain lore — *Crestone Needle, Crestone Peak* (the final Colorado fourteener to be climbed), *Ellingwood Peak.*

Yet not all who venture into the Sangres are in search of death-defying feats of mountaineering. Thousands of anglers are lured by isolated tarns of crystal-clear snowmelt to match wits with cutthroat and golden trout. Many others are drawn simply by the extraordinary scenery, vistas and abrupt ecological transitions from sand dunes to alpine pinnacles.

The Sangre de Cristo Range extends from northern New Mexico into central Colorado. The northern 70 miles of the range, from Blanca Peak to Poncha Springs, is under consideration for wilderness designation. At 252,000 acres, the Sangre de Cristo Wilderness Study Area is the largest unprotected roadless area in Colorado. If designated as wilderness, this area would be the second-largest wilderness in the state, exceeded only by the Weminuche Wilderness in the San Juans.

The name *Sangre de Cristo,* "Blood of Christ," was bestowed upon the range in 1647 as Juan De Onate and his conquistadors searched for the Seven Cities of Cibola. A priest, struck by an arrow, reportedly exclaimed "sangre de Cristo" as he lay dying, looking at the red autumn scrub oak leaves of the range's slopes. Others avow the appellation refers to the deep red hues that color the range at sunset.

Many in Colorado might assume that a magnificent and renowned feature such as the Sangre de Cristos would already be under protection. Unfortunately, the Sangres are open to assault by oil and gas development and by motor vehicles. Oil and gas companies pushing for access to explore for carbon dioxide have requested leases to the very summit of the Sangre divide. All-terrain vehicles and motorcycles make use of many of the area's trails. Hard work will be necessary to strike a compromise between providing areas for motorized use and protecting the fragile high country from the ruts, erosion, noise and pollution that can accompany motor vehicles.

Above: Morning light and rock walls above Macey Lakes   Right: Waterfall along North Colony Creek

Above: Winter sun warms frigid peaks of the Sangre de Cristo Range, from the Wet Mountains
Right: Parry primrose wildflowers precede falls along Macey Creek

GREENHORN MOUNTAIN

Size: 24,100 acres
Elevation: 7,600 to 12,367 feet
Flora: Piñon/juniper, ponderosa pine, spruce/fir, alpine tundra
Fauna: Pine marten, bighorn sheep, elk, deer, northern three-toed woodpecker, cutthroat trout
Uncommon species: Greenback cutthroat trout, possibly peregrine falcon
San Isabel National Forest

Towns in Colorado frequently have a favorite, nearby mountain retreat. For many residents of Pueblo, Greenhorn Mountain fills that niche. The focal point of the southern Front Range, Greenhorn Mountain forms the mountain backdrop to Pueblo, much as Mount Evans and Longs Peak do for cities farther north. On scorching southern Colorado summer days, Greenhorn Mountain draws the eyes and lures the heart with cool mountain breezes and carefree frolics.

The Greenhorn Mountain area is rugged, broken country dissected by numerous canyons and ridges. A road gives easy access to the Wet Mountain divide, but other than this road and a trail or two, Greenhorn Mountain is truly wild. Greenhorn Mountain and the Wet Mountain Range rise sharply to reward travelers across the Great Plains with their first dose of the Rocky Mountains. This sharp elevation gain creates a wide range of ecological life zones and attendant wildlife communities, as piñon/juniper forests give way to ponderosa, spruce and ultimately, alpine tundra. Not surprisingly, hikers who scale Greenhorn's summit are rewarded with extraordinary views of the Sangre de Cristos to the west and the vast undulations of the Great Plains to the east.

There currently exists no designated wilderness along Colorado's southern Front Range. Pueblo lies farther from its nearest wilderness than does any other major city in Colorado. Even Greeley, more often thought of as a plains community, is nearer protected mountain wildlands than is Pueblo. Greenhorn Mountain furnishes Pueblo with a backyard wilderness for the enjoyment of its citizenry and puts it on par with Colorado's other metropolitan centers.

Above: Old snag catches evening light below Greenhorn Mountain
Right: Autumn color on the flanks of Greenhorn Mountain, with the Sierra Blanca Massif in the distance

WEST NEEDLES AND WEMINUCHE ADDITIONS

Size: 31,000 acres
Elevation: 8,000 to 13,100 feet
Flora: Engelmann spruce, aspen, grassland
Fauna: Elk, deer, mountain goat, bighorn sheep, black bear, pine marten, trout
Uncommon species: None
San Juan National Forest

The West Needle Mountains stand alone as an isolated fragment of the San Juans. They appear almost as a medieval castle, stone ramparts thrust high into the skies, with deep and formidable moats — Lime Creek and the Animas River — surrounding the fortress.

The Twilight Peaks form the heart of the West Needles. These extremely steep, jagged peaks rise more than 5,000 feet above the Animas River Gorge and the route of the Durango & Silverton Narrow Gauge Railroad, dominating the landscape from Highway 550 north of Durango. Tarns of ice-blue water guard the approaches to the craggy and broken peaks. A thousand-foot cascade tumbles from Crater Lake to its union with Lime Creek in the deep valley below.

Mountain goats have been introduced into the West Needles, one of the few places in Colorado where they can be found. Mountain goats are not native to the area, but were brought in to develop additional hunting opportunities for Colorado sportsmen.

The West Needles roadless area comprises approximately 22,000 of the 31,000 acres considered for wilderness designation. The remaining acreage is distributed in three small parcels adjacent to the Weminuche Wilderness. Needle Creek is a sliver that would unite the Crazy Woman Gulch unit of the Weminuche with the main body of the wilderness. Needle Creek extends a mile both vertically and horizontally, crossing the dramatic Needle Creek valley and trail from Needleton into Chicago Basin. The tiny Weminuche Contiguous unit includes Highland Mary Lakes southeast of Silverton. Whitehead Gulch covers a portion of the Grenadier Range that is highly prominent from Molas Pass. These jigsaw puzzle pieces fill the missing gaps in the Weminuche Wilderness.

Above: Autumn aspen trees color the landscape between Lime Creek and the Twilight Peaks   Right: Snowden
Peak looms high above formations of eroded sandstone   Overleaf: Twilight Peaks earn their name

PIEDRA

Size: 60,000 acres
Elevation: 6,800 to 10,500 feet
Flora: Douglas fir, Engelmann spruce, ponderosa pine, aspen
Fauna: Elk, deer, black bear, mountain lion, pine marten, trout
Uncommon species: River otter, peregrine falcon, potentially wolverine
San Juan National Forest

Mention old-growth forests, and thoughts turn immediately to the Pacific Northwest. Colorado, too, is home to old-growth forests, and one of the finest remaining examples is in the Piedra country of the San Juan Mountains. Colorado's old growth differs greatly from that of the Northwest, owing to higher elevation, lower rainfall and poorer soils. But this is not to say that Colorado's forest patriarchs are any less magnificent.

The Piedra is an anomaly among Colorado wilderness. There are no rocks, no ice, no peaks, no lakes — nothing but thousands of acres of pristine forests and clear mountain streams. Because of its forests, the Piedra has always drawn the eye of timber companies, but has been spared clear-cuts in deference to its highly erosive and unstable soils. The Piedra remains to this day much as it might have appeared to Fathers Dominguez and Escalante in 1776 when they passed through the area at the beginning of their quest to find the Pacific Ocean. They gave the river the sonorous name *Rio de la Piedra Parada*.

The Piedra has become the focus of intense controversy over timber sales in recent years. The Forest Service has proposed to log some of the area's finest old growth along a ridge called Sandbench. Chainsaws are revved and raring to proceed, but the pending wilderness designation of adjacent lands inside the Piedra Wilderness Study Area has thus far prevented logging.

Just as delightful as the Piedra's peaceful, sun-dappled forests are the rushing waters and raging chasms of the Piedra River. Intrepid boaters brave two box canyons, narrow whitewater slots and woolly, exploding waves. Taking a breather in the slack water between adrenalin-boosting rapids, boaters may spy river otters, a native Colorado endangered species that was reintroduced to the Piedra in the 1970s. These features, and the surrounding forests, persuaded the Forest Service to propose the Piedra for designation under the federal Wild and Scenic Rivers Act.

The Piedra poses one of Colorado's most exciting wilderness opportunities — the chance to join 60,000 acres of river, pristine streams and forests to the mighty peaks of the backbone of the San Juan Mountains in the nearby Weminuche Wilderness. A wilderness corridor — a critical migration route for elk — connects the Piedra to the Weminuche. Despite decades of logging, this neck of land retains its primitive character across the few narrow miles between the two areas. When combined, the protected wilderness exceeds 500,000 acres, placing it on a par with nationally renowned wilderness ecosystems in Yellowstone, Glacier and the Sierras.

Above: The Piedra River cascades through ancient, undeveloped forests of spruce, fir and pine
Right: Red bark of a lone pine tree complements greens of the forest, along the Piedra River

SPANISH PEAKS

Size: 19,600 acres
Elevation: 8,400 to 13,626 feet
Flora: Ponderosa pine, Douglas fir, Engelmann spruce, bristlecone pine, alpine and subalpine vegetation
Fauna: Bighorn sheep, elk, deer, pine marten, northern three-toed woodpecker
Uncommon species: None
San Isabel National Forest

Crossing the vast prairie of southeastern Colorado, pioneers first glimpsed the Rockies as the pale outline of a peak or two sailing above the far western horizon. Gradually, the peaks coalesced in form and detail into the twins called the Spanish Peaks. The Spanish Peaks served as prairie beacons because of their unique position as the easternmost extension of the Rocky Mountains. Long ago, volcanic activity pushed West Spanish Peak to 13,626 feet and split its seams to create a radiating pattern of volcanic dikes. The dikes form freestanding walls, some more than 100 feet in height, and extend across the Cuchara Valley as far as 14 miles from their source in the peaks. In line, form and texture, the dikes abruptly break the landscape. As acknowledgement of the area's unique geology, the Spanish Peaks were designated as a national natural landmark in 1977.

Designation as a national natural landmark offers recognition to an area, but affords none of the protective attributes of wilderness designation. Leases to explore for carbon dioxide in the Spanish Peaks have been requested by four companies. Much of the Spanish Peaks consists of steep slopes with sparse vegetation and is poorly situated for the extensive road cuts and drill pads that accompany oil and gas exploration.

The Spanish Peaks are known locally by their Indian name, *Wahatoya*, or its Spanish-language equivalent, *Huajatolla*. Wahatoya translates to a more visually descriptive name for the peaks, "Breasts of the World."

Above: Hundred-foot-high volcanic dikes radiate from the Spanish Peaks
Right: Evening light bathes sparse vegetation below West Spanish Peak

Above: Autumn's aspen manifest both color and detail in cloudy light
Right: West Spanish Peak reappears after an autumn snowstorm

SOUTH SAN JUAN ADDITIONS

Size: 32,800 acres
Elevation: 8,200 to 13,000 feet
Flora: Engelmann spruce, aspen, alpine tundra
Fauna: Elk, deer, black bear, turkey, bighorn sheep, trout
Uncommon species: Potentially grizzly bear and wolverine
San Juan National Forest

On a late fall day in 1979, Colorado's last known grizzly was killed at the head of the Navajo River. Grizzlies were thought to be long extinct from Colorado, but a lonely sow grizzly apparently survived through the years in this remote corner of the state. An intensive search for more grizzlies was launched by the Colorado Division of Wildlife, but none were found.

The Navajo River originates in the South San Juan Wilderness. This 133,463-acre wilderness was designated by Congress in 1980, but during congressional discussion no resolution was reached on the fate of some 33,000 acres of contiguous roadless lands. Two areas were left for further study: Montezuma Peak, 13,000 acres at the head of the San Juan River, and V-Rock Trail, 19,800 acres west of the Navajo River.

Bordered by the Continental Divide, Montezuma Peak is an area of stereotypical Colorado mountain splendor — steep slopes, alpine lakes and cascading streams. Montezuma Peak also contains appearances of geologic alterations typical of economic mineralization. As a result, it attracts mineral prospectors as well as mountain connoisseurs. This potential interest in mining, molybdenum in particular, is what caused Montezuma Peak to be left for further wilderness study in 1980. Mining interest has faded in the intervening years.

The distinctive outline of V-Rock catches the eye immediately upon glancing at a topographic map. The area roughly follows the watershed divide between the Navajo River and the Rio Blanco, creating a long, narrow appendage to the South San Juan Wilderness. V-Rock Trail traverses its length, paralleling the Chalk Mountains. Timber and oil were the extractive resources of interest here in 1980, but with the closure of a nearby timber mill and the lack of production from a small local oil field, there appears to be little serious conflict with wilderness designation today. Though Colorado's last known grizzly disappeared more than a decade ago, her habitat along the Navajo River headwaters in V-Rock can still be preserved through swift action.

Above: Sunset reflects into a tundra pool below Montezuma Peak   Right: Aspen penetrate the fog of a fast-moving storm in the Chalk Mountains   Overleaf: Predawn below Montezuma Peak

JOHN FIELDER

ADDITIONAL ISSUES

Wilderness Water Rights

Of all the wilderness myths in Colorado, the wilderness water rights myth has the least to do with reality, but the most to do with stalling a Colorado wilderness bill for nearly a decade.

The water that is natural to wilderness shapes it, nourishes it, gives it meaning. When we set aside wilderness, should we also protect enough of that water to preserve the wilderness values that relate to it? The obvious answer is yes. But some interests have seized on the water issue as a new anti-wilderness tool. They claim a federal wilderness water right would damage private rights, disrupt the state's system for managing water rights and foreclose future economic development in Colorado. It would do none of these things.

A federal wilderness water right declares that the public is entitled to protection of public water on public land — wilderness, for example. It declares that in their damming, diverting and draining of Colorado's streams and rivers decades into the future, developers must take into account the presence of wilderness and its right to enough water to give it meaning.

Wilderness does not consume water. The water that rises in wilderness flows out again — cleanly, reliably and available for human use. A wilderness water right demands only that wild streams and rivers be allowed to flow where they have always flowed, to serve our few remaining wild places.

There is nothing remarkable and not much new about such protection of wilderness water. While the debate has raged in Colorado, while wilderness has been lost in the interim, Congress has four times designated wilderness in other western states. The compromise provisions have become almost commonplace:

- Wilderness is entitled to enough water, and only enough water, to protect wilderness purposes.
- A federal wilderness water right must come from water not already spoken for by private right holders.
- A federal wilderness water right must be claimed wholly within the state's water rights system.
- A federal wilderness water right dates from the day the wilderness designation is signed into law and takes its place in line behind all rights that are senior or older.

Senator Tim Wirth's wilderness bill follows these provisions. Representative Ben Nighthorse Campbell's proposal is similar in many respects. Senator Bill Armstrong's bill flatly declares that there can be no federal water right on behalf of either existing or proposed Colorado wilderness.

Under Colorado water law, a person acquires the right to use water by diverting it from a stream for "beneficial use." Such use includes water for drinking, irrigation and industry. Whoever claims the water first gets the right to use it first. In times of shortage, those with newer rights may receive no water.

As a practical matter, water flowing naturally in a stream is not considered to be a beneficial use under Colorado water law. In 1973, the Colorado General Assembly enacted a law to ". . . appropriate . . . or acquire such waters of natural streams or lakes as may be required to preserve the natural environment to a reasonable degree." The law vested the Colorado Water Conservation Board with authority for this protection under what has come to be known as the "instream flow program." While the language of the statute is broad, in practice the board does not claim more than the water needed to protect a coldwater fishery — "fish flows" as they are called. Clearly, wilderness needs more than that — for wildlife, wetlands, plants, scenery, science, recreation.

Even if the state water board claimed enough water for the full range of wilderness values, it would be no substitute for a

Above: Climax molybdenum mine, near Leadville
Opposite: Orange sneezeweed, South San Juan Additions

75

water right held by the federal land manager and enforceable on behalf of the American people whose wilderness this is. The state legislature that created the instream flow program could abolish it tomorrow. If wilderness is to be an "enduring resource" as Congress declared in the Wilderness Act of 1964, its protections, too, must be permanent. The proper tool for ensuring that permanence is a federal wilderness water right.

The anti-wilderness forces — the Colorado Farm Bureau, the water development community and others — rest much of their argument against a wilderness water right for headwaters on the claim that water protection for headwater areas would set a precedent for designations yet to come on lands administered by the Bureau of Land Management (BLM). It is useful to understand the geography of this debate. Headwater areas — such as all those included in the Wirth bill — are those whose streams originate inside proposed wilderness boundaries. Thus, upstream from the wilderness there is no private or non-wilderness federal land where new water diversions could occur. As a result, there are no conflicts between wilderness protection and future water development in these headwater areas.

Old truck, Lost Creek Wilderness

Some BLM lands that are wilderness candidates are, indeed, downstream of either private or non-wilderness public lands — lands where new water diversions could occur. The presence of a wilderness area — with a water right — downstream from these lands could complicate future diversions. But wilderness opponents have grossly exaggerated the potential conflicts. First,

the BLM itself notes that among the dozens of candidate areas, no more than eight or nine are "downstream areas" by definition. Most of the proposed BLM wilderness areas are headwater areas in the context of this debate. Two such areas contain two of Colorado's famous 14,000-foot mountains — Redcloud and Sunshine peaks.

Where conflicts do exist, they can be dealt with case by case as all conflicts between wilderness designation and development proposals have always been dealt with since the Wilderness Act itself was passed more than 25 years ago. Evidence for this proposition is found in the recent congressional enactments referred to previously. Four times in recent years — while developers have held a Colorado wilderness bill hostage over water rights — Congress has moved to protect western wildlands and the water that belongs to them. Some of these areas are far downstream from their headwaters. Each time, Congress has settled on water language very similar to the language Senator Wirth has proposed. Each time, the language gained the acceptance of the state's congressional delegation and of the state's water authorities. Remarkably enough, such agreements have been achieved in Nevada and Arizona, states even more arid than our own and with similar state water laws.

There is no reason not to protect our headwater wilderness areas now. And there is no reason not to believe that we cannot do what other western states have done: deal with downstream areas when it is time to deal with them using the principles Congress has established for wilderness water rights.

Off-Road Vehicular Traffic

Two facts stand out: motorized vehicles are not allowed in wilderness areas, and Colorado's heritage is grounded in the industries of mining, ranching and farming. One of the legacies of the mining industry, as well as the timber industry, is a vast network of back-country roads. In fact, there are 35,000 miles of roads through national forest land in Colorado. In addition, more than *five million* acres of BLM land in Colorado are available for cross-country and off-highway use.

Improved and unimproved roads take us into any kind of scenery we would ever wish to visit. From the semi-arid deserts of the Great Plains of eastern Colorado to the alpine zone high above treeline in the San Juan Mountains, these old highways of sheepherders and miners allow us quick, easy access with sturdy four-wheel drives, motorcycles or go-anywhere ATVs. In fact, Colorado enjoys the most extensive network of mountain back roads in the world.

Some people insist that we need more of these roads and support the argument that more timbering means more roads for recreation. Others say that these fragile mountain trails, used historically by both pedestrians and motorcycles alike, should sustain both uses despite a clear danger that misuse and overuse by machines erodes trails into uselessness. Others deny that the noise of motorized vehicles compromises one of the essences of wilderness — its solitude.

In the Armstrong bill and the Campbell proposal, the entire Fossil Ridge Wilderness Study Area has been ignored, mostly because historical precedent has allowed motorcycle use on its trails. Fossil Ridge is a pristine wild area, and its flora and fauna deserve solitude befitting its wildness. For many years the remarkable Rainbow Trail of the Sangre de Cristo Range has endured motorized traffic. Unfortunately, so have numerous side trails — which are legally off-limits to vehicles — that penetrate the fragile subalpine environs of these mountains. What a shame it is that only the Wirth bill protects much of this trail from the noise and pollution of the combustion engine.

Why do we need to erode these footpaths intended for hardy souls seeking the joy of physical exercise and the elixir of hearing only birds singing and creeks gurgling? Do we not have enough well-worn roads, which by their very definition accommodate tire traffic? Are not the thousands of their miles over passes named long ago — Engineer and Georgia and Black Bear and a hundred others — enough to satisfy our wanderlust in and on those machines that save the legs? I think so, for I have traveled just about them all and know quite well what is to be seen beside them and beyond. Often the sights are as pretty as can be viewed in even wilderness lands.

Some have said wilderness is only for the elite, ostensibly because a person must be hardy and cerebral to enjoy remote places. Yet the cost of some four-wheel-drive vehicles, and the expense plowed back into them on accessories to make them more useful, is so great that I wonder if this pastime of driving nature's back roads is not elitist. Most backpackers I know spend hundreds of dollars, most four-wheelers thousands.

Boundary Considerations

A quick look at the total acreages in Colorado's three wilderness proposals shows that each man has his own idea as to what qualifies as wilderness. Senator Wirth's bill contains 751,260 acres of proposed wilderness, Representative Campbell's proposal has 641,410 acres and Senator Armstrong's bill has 471,875 acres.

There are numerous reasons why there are such gaps among the proposals. As mentioned previously, Fossil Ridge has been left out of two of the three proposals because of historical off-road vehicle use. Although the Oh! Be Joyful proposed wilderness lies contiguous with the existing Raggeds Wilderness, and though it is as pristine an alpine valley as there exists anywhere, it lies only one mile from the Mount Emmons molybdenum deposit. Designating Oh! Be Joyful merely as a national recreation area would not protect it from mining.

The Forest Service contends there are too many "external influences" on the Saint Louis Peak portion of the Saint Louis and Vasquez peaks proposed wilderness, yet it is as wild and scenic as the Vasquez portion. Likewise, the Williams Fork proposed wilderness has been discounted from one bill because of more water diversion plans in this area as laid out by the Denver Water Board. Without wilderness protection, the area's wonderfully dense forests of spruce, fir, pine and aspen would be invaded by miles of diversion canals.

These latter two areas are of particular importance because of their proximity to Front Range communities. More wilderness is sorely needed to take the pressure off overused areas such as the existing Indian Peaks and Mount Evans wildernesses. The proposed addition to the Lost Creek Wilderness also fits into this category. And areas such as American Flats and Williams Fork are close to roads that would make more wilderness accessible to the elderly or the physically challenged.

We are quick to forget that there are at least 10 million acres of roadless land in Colorado, land that could qualify as wilderness if it were not for minor alterations by man — alterations that nature will shortly reclaim anyway. Yet we are now considering proposals that at most would designate 781,280 acres. In this context we must again consider the most important question: is an additional 1 percent, above the existing 4 percent, a great enough percentage of Colorado to maintain the biological and economic needs of the state for future generations?

Clear-cutting, below the Lost Creek Wilderness

Conclusion

The Saint Louis skier cruising through fresh powder snow at Winter Park may not come back to Colorado if he must look at clear-cut ridges in the Saint Louis and Vasquez peaks proposed wilderness. The elk hunter from Dallas may not be tempted to relocate if, on his vacations, he must sight his rifle across mine tailings to get his trophy.

The future economic health of Colorado is based upon two factors — the success of the tourism and recreation industry and the quality of life that we can offer to prospective residents. Maximizing tourism and recreation is a function of preserving and protecting Colorado's last remaining wildlands, molding Colorado's image as a place of wildness and marketing that image. Our appeal to the denizens of cities around the country and the world is that Colorado is a place where they can retreat from the pressures of urban society. We must protect our wildlands from overuse by managing them wisely. Tourism is a sustainable industry, with a guarantee of hundreds of thousands of jobs for years to come, if only we do not deplete our most valuable assets — our mountains, our plains and our river canyons.

By creating more open space in our cities and towns, by protecting the wildness of the most natural places and by increasing the potential for recreational use of our open lands, our high quality of life in Colorado will attract business as never before. That fact in itself will guarantee jobs for our children and theirs for decades to come. We must act now, for the development of natural and open lands continues at a rapid pace. The wilderness issue cannot be decided in 10 years or even five, for by then it will certainly be too late. We, the people of Colorado, must decide now.

Wilderness is for people, without a doubt. But it has value whether we walk through it, just go to its edges and peer in, simply rejoice in the knowledge that it exists . . . or never even spare it a thought. Wilderness is far more than a recreational resource to be allocated among competing users. We may recreate in it, we may use it to restore our spirits, but when we do, we must do it in a way that protects the very values we have come to see. Recreation is an appropriate use of wilderness but is not the only, and not even the most important use. Wilderness serves as a natural treasure house,

where natural systems can operate naturally and, to the extent possible, without man's interference. This fact alone may ensure mankind's survival. Wilderness serves as a standard against which we can measure the impact of our actions on the world we live in. Wilderness is its own reason for being; our direct use of it is secondary.

If humans control the destiny of the earth, then just knowing that wilderness exists may dictate that destiny. Whether we visit wilderness or not, are we not more secure just in the knowledge that there is a natural place to retreat to? On those Wednesdays when the burden of making a living climaxes and we daydream of a weekend sojourn to the hills, isn't that thought often enough to see us through the week? The simple knowledge that wildness exists may be infinitely more important than any visit, for it calms our spirits, allays the chaos in our lives and makes us feel secure as residents of our planet. And wisdom surely will follow.

— JOHN FIELDER

COMPARISONS OF WILDERNESS PROPOSAL ACREAGES

Common Name (North to South)	Wirth	Armstrong	Campbell
Davis Peak (Mount Zirkel Addition)	36,000	9,800	14,400
Service Creek	54,700	33,600	43,200
Saint Louis and Vasquez peaks	24,160	11,300	24,000
Williams Fork	40,000	55,100(NRA)	53,900
Lost Creek Addition	11,000	7,000	11,000
Spruce Creek (Hunter–Fryingpan Addition)	8,000	8,000	8,000
Buffalo Peaks	58,160	29,400	43,800
Oh! Be Joyful (Raggeds Addition)	5,500	5,500(NRA)	5,500
Fossil Ridge	55,560	43,300(NRA)	0
Roubideau	0	0	19,780
Tabeguache	0	0	10,240
Cannibal Plateau–Powderhorn	69,940	62,300	62,300
Big Blue Additions	3,900	1,200	2,330
Wheeler Geologic (La Garita Addition)	25,000	15,900	15,900
Sangre de Cristo	252,080	195,100	230,000
Greenhorn Mountain	24,130	22,000	22,000
West Needles and Weminuche Additions	30,760	23,975	23,860
Piedra	60,000 (WSA)	41,500	41,500(WSA)
Spanish Peaks	19,570	18,400(NRA)	18,400
South San Juan Additions	32,800	10,800	32,800
ACTUAL WILDERNESS ACREAGE	751,260	471,875	641,410
ACRES DESIGNATED AS NRAs	0	122,300	0
ACRES LEFT IN STUDY STATUS (WSA)	60,000	0	41,500

WSA: Wilderness Study Area

NRA: National Recreation Area

DAVID LAVENDER

AFTERWORD

Not long ago, while driving through the rumpled countryside of a lumbering region in a neighboring state, I grew aware of an ideological battle being waged by means of bumper stickers. The message carried by approximately one car in 20 read WILDERNESS, LAND OF NO USE. The rejoinder was delivered by about one car in 50: WILDERNESS, LAND OF NO ABUSE.

The opposed contentions, admirably distilled, represent a familiar donnybrook. How should the last unexploited lands of this high-tech nation be treated? Considering where I was when I made my rough estimate, it is not surprising that the odds were 5 to 2 in favor of using adding machines to judge life's quality. These odds are a persistent carry-over of our frontier mind-set, *frontier* being identified here as the constantly advancing points where our pioneers kept re-encountering the New World's vast lottery — a whole continent up for grabs.

West. Old West. Synonyms for *bonanza*. Take what you wanted, legally or otherwise, and milk it for all it was worth. It was wonderful, a challenge to our pioneers' ingenuity, endurance and strength. Such feats deserved to be rewarded. And we deserve to share the laurels. For, by extension, we too are conquerors of the land and of whatever nations and races stood in our way.

Our great expectations turned us, in the quaint phrase of one English philosopher, into "end gainers." In today's snappier business jargon, the words would be translated into "goal oriented." We were — are — in pursuit of products. In our hurry to achieve — what a complimentary term we consider the word *achiever* to be! — we forget to pay attention to the side effects of attaining our heart's desires. We scarcely notice, for example, the huge, rusty-gray waste dump outside the black mouth of nearly every abandoned mine tunnel in Colorado.

(Take a look at Fryer Hill back of Leadville. Hey, man, the bonanza boys siphoned *millions* out of those holes! For kicks they added the legend of H.A.W. Tabor. They sighed over Baby Doe as a warning against pride and misplaced love. But no sighs for the land. Millions! Who grieves over that?)

Today we do notice, briefly in passing, corkscrewing road scars leading toward the grotesque blotches of clear-cuts in once handsomely unbroken carpets of evergreens. But how much attention do we pay to the processes of erosion the clear-cuts launch, or to the retreat of tormented wildlife — yup, the good old spotted owl again?

(Take a gander at the machinery the loggers use. Impressive! And costly. The bonanza companies could hardly pay for so much high-tech implementation if the Forest Service did not obligingly sell the trees at less than cost. Forest Service. Do people recall 1960, when Congress passed the "Multiple Use–Sustained Yield" bill? Whatever happened to the second part of that slogan? *Sustained Yield*: keep those words in mind. Ah, well, desolation means jobs, at least for a while. So slap the sticker onto the car's bumper and ride merrily on to the next cut.)

In view of the enormous environmental problems facing the entire world, additional wilderness areas in Colorado may seem unworthy of the fuss they are getting here. For how can they possibly matter compared to deficiencies in the ozone layer, to global warming, to the siting of nuclear waste dumps, to the pollution not just of streams and lakes but of oceans and the atmosphere itself?

If you simply use your calculator to add up acreage, you are not going to get much of an argument. In terms of mind-set, however, the acres may become part of an infinitely important revolution.

What we are now facing — what we let come out of our collective subconscious during our multitude of Earth Day celebrations — is what Professor Donella Meadows of Dartmouth College has called mankind's third great upheaval. The first great revolution — *revolution* being used in the sense of a complete turnaround in our ways of perception — was agriculture. It introduced primitive people to the idea of confining most of their work to pieces of private property. It made possible booming population growth. In turn this fostered the idea of specialized labor — not just the hunters and gatherers of old, but potters, artists, priests and, in arid areas, designers and managers of irrigation systems.

Next, many millennia later, came the industrial revolution, which imposed a mind-set on us that is proving almost impossible to shake off. Here the new idea was to combine capital and technology in such ways that we were able to produce every commodity, money included, that we could have possibly wanted, plus lots more that we neither wanted nor needed. As long as the resources of earth, water and air seemed unlimited, we felt no need to worry about the side effects we were releasing as we achieved. As a consequence the world became, in many places, an unsightly mess.

Now we are learning that the three basics — earth, water, air — are not unlimited. We are learning at last, it is to be hoped, that we do need to pay attention to side effects, for they are becoming the main effects, often through sheer carelessness, of our tremendous material achievements. Most of all, we are belatedly coming to realize that we must *sustain* what we have because there is no more.

Sustained yield. Congress mumbled the words once and then forgot. Now we must remember. Working out the concept of sustained yield as it applies to every item in our daily living has to be mankind's third great revolution. It is not an easy concept for a people whose minds are set to the values of the industrial revolution.

This is where wilderness comes in. It is, in the narrowest sense, a vital way of sustaining the natural jewels we have. In a broader sense, wilderness can help us develop the concepts of sustained yield that the planet must have if it is to survive.

I have a friend, a teacher of high school students, who every so often takes teenagers on overnight — sometimes multiple-night — backpacking, canoe or horseback camping trips. He goes into congressionally designated wilderness areas whenever he can reach them. If for some reason circumstances prevent this, he manages to substitute some quiet pool or rustling stand of shrubs that is big enough for life to present itself in headier ways than it does on city streets.

My friend never talks about going into the land. He talks about the land coming to his young explorers and to him. That ruddy cliff out yonder — they don't reach it. Rather, Kurt wants them to turn their perceptions around. He wants them to sense, as they walk, paddle or ride, that it is flowing toward them with its gifts at a leisurely two and a half miles an hour. That way they get to greet it.

A distinction without a difference? Not to Kurt. He is trying to instill an awareness of the difference between taking and receiving. Our pioneers took. In many cases they grew rich. But they spoiled. Nowadays we need to receive — openly, gladly — and in a different way grow still richer, for we will be sustaining, not grabbing.

Currently I am working on a book about Indians, and I have come to believe that they didn't grab because they lacked the technology that would have enabled them to do so. They received, with no desire to subdue any more of nature than they needed to sustain their lives. Sky, earth, water, sun, grass, trees, heat and cold, game and fish drifted to them, combined into a seamless experience. Having killed, they thanked the spirit of the killed for taking care of them. Life was a gift they kept receiving over and over. Do we pay tribute to the deaths we cause? Hardly. But we may learn to if we have to sustain the world that supports us.

Wilderness may help us learn. For it will provide us with legally constituted islands of stability in an increasingly bewildered, increasingly lawless world. It will provide sanctuaries for our hearts, sanctuaries where the pulse of time beats with its old, sure rhythms, and the unsullied blueness of space remains as an emblem of all those gifts that will someday lie beyond the reach of taking for exploitation's sake. Maybe, just maybe, this view of wilderness will expand into a revolutionary new mind-set that will have us paying attention to the destruction we are creating.

Thoreau sensed this long ago. We can't repeat often enough what he said: "In wildness is the salvation of the world." In order to receive that salvation, we must revolt. One way is to increase the number of wilderness areas still available. It may be our last chance.

— DAVID LAVENDER